Walk the Talk: Africa / Asia Focus

Report of the International Online Conferences

January/ March 2021

Organized by

*Geneva Agape Foundation with World Council of Churches,
FaithInvest, World Evangelical Alliance Business Coalition, Uniapac*

Walk the Talk: Africa / Asia Focus

Report of the International Online Conference

January / March 2021

Globethics.net Agape Series No. 6

GAF Agape Series at Globethics.net.

Publications Director: Prof. Dr Obiora Ike, Executive Director of Globethics.net in Geneva and Professor of Ethics at the Godfrey Okoye University Enugu/ Nigeria.

Series Editor: Prof. Dr Dr h.c. Christoph Stückelberger. Founder and President of Globethics.net and Professor of Ethics, University of Basel/Switzerland

Globethics.net Agape Series 6

Walk the Talk. Africa / Asia Focus. Report of the International Online Conference, Jan / Mar 2021, Geneva: GAF, 2021.
ISBN 978-2-88931- 411-9 (online version)
ISBN 978-2-88931-412-6 (print version)
© 2021 Geneva Agape Foundation
© 2021 Globethics.net

Main Author of the Report: Haicun Kong
Managing Editor: Dr Ignace Haaz
Assistant Editors: Hong Bui, Haicun Kong
Cover Design and Art: Prof. Dr Cui Wantian, China, Artist

Globethics.net
International Secretariat
150 route de Ferney
1211 Geneva 2, Switzerland
Website:
www.globethics.net/publications
Email:*publications@globethics.net*

Geneva Agape Foundation (GAF)
150 route de Ferney
1211 Geneva 2, Switzerland
Website:
https://gafoundation.world/en/publications
Email: info@gafoundation.world

All web links in this text have been verified as of May 2021.

The electronic version of this book can be downloaded for free and print copies ordered at https://www.globethics.net/agape-series

CONTENTS

Quote From Speakers   **7**

1 Introduction   **11**

2 Summary:Walk the Talk - Africa Focus   **13**

3 Conference Recommendations - Africa Focus   **16**

4 Summary: Walk the Talk - Asia Focus   **19**

5 Conference Recommendations - Asia Focus   **23**

Appendices   **26**

Conference Programme: Africa-Focus *26*

Conference Programme: Asia-Focus *28*

Speakers and Participants Africa-Focus *30*

Speakers and Participants Asia-Focus *32*

Photo Gallery *34*

Most of the conference presentations can be downloaded for free here:
https://gafoundation.world/en/conference/conference-2021

Resources for the topic of the conference can be found among others on
GAF Publications:
https://gafoundation.world/en/publications
GAF Directories of Christian Entrepreneurs
https://gafoundation.world/en/programmes/programme-3/project-2-
faithinvest-cooperation-with-gaf
GAF Directory of Faith-driven Investments
https://gafoundation.world/en/programmes/programme-3/project-3-
values-driven-investment-directory

QUOTE FROM SPEAKERS

At the closing of the 2021 faith-driven investing, Walk the Talk Conference, the wide consensus reached by participants was to work together in the spirit of the conference that reflects the following points:

"We faced dramatic impact of COVID-19 around the world from the end of 2019. It brings us new challenges but also, meanwhile, it brings diverse opportunities for investment. We want to mobilize the spiritual side, faith-driven we say, sharing our resources and knowledge to ensure the potential investors." *Christoph Stückelberger, Executive Director of Geneva Agape Foundation, President of Globethics.net Foundation, President of OikosInvest Foundation, Professor emeritus of Ethics and visiting Professor in UK, Nigeria, Russia, China.*

"There are lessons to be seriously taken; health issues are warning us that economy and ecology cannot be treated separately. We are all inter-connected as one community and the health of our neighbors impacts our own directly, which we can see from this pandemic moment. We need to invest deeply in a system of healthcare resilience and social sustainability." *Isabel Phiri, Deputy General Secretary at World Council of Churches, Geneva, Switzerland.*

"The change in the world globally, during 2020, has made such a significant difference. But there are always opportunities when the world changes." *Anis Asghar, Founder of Clan Capital an investment-based company in London and Chief Investment Officer of UNGSII.*

"Do we each want to be the best in the world, or do we want to be the best for the world? We do indeed need a change of paradigm, I say P square seven: public private partnerships for people, planet, purpose, and profit ... If we can align all of those 7 'P's', we can succeed. It is brilliant introduction of this conference which suggests we should Walk the Talk. I cannot agree more but I humbly suggest we replace Walk the Talk with Run the Talk in order to boost the transformation of finance at the creation of innovation partnerships. We have no time, and we really need to transit from this present business organizing into a new paradigm." *Nicholas Niggli, Deputy Secretary General at the Republic and State of Geneva.*

"We, Africans, live on a continent that already has a fragile healthcare system. The healthcare system is already over stretched on its knees. Definitely, this pandemic brought in new challenges ...Therefore, under the pandemic COVID-19, we have various opportunities for innovation in a lot of areas. One of them is leadership and governance. We need to change the way we work with people and the virtual governance models. We also have opportunities in health management especially, in information systems." *Nkatha Njeru, Church perspective. African Christian Health Association ACHA.*

"It is particularly noticeable that over the past 3 years, Chinese investment in the energy part, particularly the alternative energy or renewable energy, such as solar, wind power, or hydro has increased significantly from 39% to 51%." *Baocheng Liu, Professor of Business Ethics, Beijing, China.*

"I think faith-based is something of a challenge here. Because you might have certain ideals involved in the investment activities, then you should go through it and put all the commitment you have. You are willing to take all different burdens. Eventually, it become a proven concept." *Prune (Phakdiphibul) Ansvananda, UNIAPAC's Regional President for Asia and Chairman of Catholic Business Executives Group (a club formed by Thailand's leading Catholic business professionals).*

"I hope, in Japan, the generation can change within the faith-based organizations. These organizations can guide the Japanese and provide the simple guideline for faith-based investment, which is telling people what and how we the Japanese can proceed with faith-based investment." *Mizue Tsukushi, President and CEO of The Good Bankers Co., Ltd., is a Pioneer in implementing SRI products into the Japanese market.*

"We have assisted the great entrepreneurs who have settled those companies which along with SDGs, for example supplying the local people or giving everyone access to water and sanitation, but also on the other SDGs." *Jean-Pierre Sweerts, CEO of the Water Finance Facility and Chairman of the Boards of DOB Equity, The Borneo Initiative and of the Investment Committee of Energy Fund Overijssel. He is also a board member of Geneva Agape Foundation.*

"We are all human beings, and we need to motivate people to think more carefully about the choices we make and to mobilize capital and action towards faith-based investment ... Now, Africa offers us great opportunities as well as challenges." *Vivek Mittal, Hindu, CEO AfIDA (Africa Infrastructure Dev. Assoc.), India/London. AfIDA Africa is a* non-profit association of leading private sector participants in infrastructure development, finance and operations in Africa, which together have over $20 billion of capital invested in African infrastructure.

"I spell Faith is R.I.S.K" *Mason Tan, Founder Garden Impact Investments, Singapore.*

The participation from public and private sector stakeholders at high levels such as *UNIAPAC, ACHAP, WCC, UNGSII Geneva State,* etc. confirms the necessity of such an event. The participants were satisfied with the level of professionalism and diversity and innovative creativity to impact business and society. ***The next conference* is planned in Geneva at the Ecumenical Centre on January 13-15, 2022.**

All the videos are available here:
https://gafoundation.world/en/conference/conference-2021

1

INTRODUCTION

Ethical business, values-driven entrepreneurship, spiritual resourcing of businesspeople, innovative trends in responsible leadership, networking between faith-driven business leaders: these have been topics of the annual conferences of the Geneva Agape Foundation at the Ecumenical Centre in Geneva each year in January before the World Economic Forum week.

In 2021, the conference, summarised in this conference report, was different and promising in at least six aspects:

1. Due to the COVID-19 pandemic, the conference was held *online only*. Although the important face-to-face contact among participants was missing, the online platform still allowed broad participation from all continents — without travel costs and flight-related CO^2-emissions.

2. Due to time zone differences, it was organised in two one-day conferences, one in January with the *Africa-Focus* and one in March with the *Asia Focus*. Some courageous participants and speakers still joined at midnight or late night from America.

3. The conference title *"Walk the Talk"* indicated that we must go beyond talking. Action, implementation, and impact is needed. Reflection, concepts, values, inner formation are important foundations, but implementation counts. This is even truer under the painful sufferings of millions of people related to the global

pandemic catastrophe. A speaker called not only for *"walk the talk"*, but even for *"run the talk"*! It became the phrase of the day.

4. The 2021 online conferences have been co-organized by an enlarged group of *five organising institutions/networks*: the Geneva Agape Foundation in cooperation with FaithInvest, the WEA Business Coalition, the World Council of Churches and recently with Uniapac, one of the oldest global Christian entrepreneur's associations. This shows the interest and potential of cooperation. It creates synergies, mutual support and enrichment while remaining independent organisations with their specific mandates, mission, target groups and instruments.

5. As in the past, the conference mainly focused on *Christian* faith-based and values-driven entrepreneurship. However, representatives from *other faith communities* and non-faith-based backgrounds have been among speakers and participants. Including multiple perspectives was especially important in the Asia context. This interfaith approach may increase in future years.

6. From a business and faith perspective to human development, the UN Sustainable Development Goals (SDGs) remain a core framework of goals and efforts for the conference. Faith-based entrepreneurs can and do contribute a lot to place purpose before profit; to see business not only as a job, but as a vocation; to implement leadership as servant leadership; and to resist unethical business practices even under very tough pandemic-conditions by sticking to integrity and maintaining a strong inner spiritual motivation and commitment to serve humanity with the SDGs.

Geneva, May 2021

Prof. Dr Christoph Stückelberger
Executive Director Geneva Agape Foundation
Conference Moderator

2

SUMMARY:
WALK THE TALK - AFRICA FOCUS

This online session of international conference 2021, faith-driven, Walk the Talk Africa-Focus opens during this extra special moment which is seriously affected by COVID-19 worldwide. Hundreds of millions of people lost or will lose their jobs and millions of small and medium enterprises will close — this, the devastating impact. It is no doubt that COVID-19 has brought irrevocable changes to our lives and the global economy around the world.

However, how to face this situation positively and react correctly, or even how to mobilize investment on the spiritual side, is what we want to explore and gather from this conference. Hundreds of participates from different international and national associations, academic institutions, churches, public and private sectors, present these international online conferences and expect more essential changes on those issues.

"We, Africans, are living on a continent where the healthcare systems are very fragile, and this pandemic definitely brought more new challenges. However, aside from the challenges, we saw also various opportunities to mobilize the communities to supply better services. There is an urgent need of innovation from different areas such as leadership and governance, information management, technologies, cooperation strategies etc. We encourage those faith-based organizations to partner with Christian health associations and build the capacity for pursuing those opportunities mentioned before," said Nkatha Njeru from African Christian Health Association ACHA. Apparently, this is a common expression from most of the African participants.

Africa, as Mr. Bruno Bubone, President of UNIAPAC, said, is a marvelous continent, which has most of the potential wealth for our world development. On the stage of world development, Africa has the very important asset of youth and the capacity for growth. Meanwhile, we should give Africa the opportunities to become a strong contributor for world development, social resilience and environmental sustainability, especially from the impact investment point of view. As stated earlier, Africa has the great advantage of youth and capacity for growth. Another advantage is the opportunity for digitalization or new technology, which is induced by Mr. Günter Nooke from his experiences. For example, block chain technologies have the potential of greatly increasing the transparency and efficiency of economic cooperation for the investors. There is also a specific cooperate mode, so-called strategic partnership technology which means the business sectors, communities, and politics work together. It provides grants to investment that combine private and social interests.

All in all, a remarkably large consensus was reached for faith-driven investment in the context of Africa from the conferences:

2.1 Firstly, the participants of the conference are all multi-stakeholders of multi-disciplines and multi-faiths mostly from Africa, such as public parts, private sectors, faith-based organizations, churches, academic institutions, etc. This means we are making bridges for different organizations to come together with World Council of Churches, Geneva Agape Foundation and Faith-Invest. Therefore, the multi-aspects presented by the participants must be underlined.

2.2 Secondly, to solve the challenges of the pandemic mentioned during the conference, cooperation with public and the other faith-based private sectors or organizations, is what we should rely on to mobilize the local communities and providing proper services. We are all in one boat and all of us are tightly interconnected which we can see from this worldwide crisis. We need to cooperate and make connection between multi-aspect stakeholders, public sectors, private sectors, and other faith-based organisations to show the characteristic of this conference, the Africa-Europe focus. On this point of view, building trust is an essential ingredient in all of our human relations. This platform brings many stakeholders together from the private and public sectors.

2.3 Thirdly, one of the most important elements of the conference is faith-driven focus. To mobilize or to help mobilize the faith-based, or values-driven communities, it must be said that we have a lot of assets, competence and skills to contribute to the SDGs. We need to discuss how we can better link SDG implementation and global governance with the whole financing aspect. So, it is important to have both profits and good purpose, but not promote one over the other. This means creating balance between sustainability and profit maximization; aligning financial returns with social responsibility is one of the best methods for enhancing social resilience.

Obviously, in order to get on the correct road of sustainability and move further, we need to focus on faith-based organizations, or other public and private sectors to build a new business model of ethical investment.

3

CONFERENCE RECOMMENDATIONS: AFRICA FOCUS

This international online conference is focused mainly on the faith investments, churches, church related hospitals, universities and schools, etc. We need to find the resource or nature of faith in which we cooperate with all people of goodwill and values, such as hope, love, that are sometimes the precondition for investing and sharing the resource. There are lessons to be learned from this pandemic: health must be treated with economy and ecology, shared as every single person is interconnected. We must redefine completely what risks we take and radically expand our understanding of what is of value beyond financial expectation.

The purpose of this online conference is to create opportunities for those faith-based groups, investors and entrepreneurs to meet, collaborate, and act towards making a better difference for the planet we live on. Meanwhile, we are trying to improve, increase and encourage value-driving and faith-driving investment with a special focus on Africa. Numerous great ideas for faith-based investment are brought to the conference to enhance the social resilience and sustainability of Africa.

3.1 Firstly, the multi-stakeholder approach is one of the most remarkable outcomes from this conference. We need this coalition among the various organizations, institutions, NGOs, churches, public and private sectors to face to the challenges, during this period of global crisis due to COVID-19. Those challenges and opportunities cannot be well-handled without government regulations, private sector money inflow, academic knowledge, scientific activities, and especially the role of the grassroots effort, values and spirituality of faith communities

3.2 Secondly, the business model of profit and purpose is another outcome from this conference. This means the awareness of business today must combine profit with sustainable purpose. The sustainable business models require increased awareness in several different panels which are necessary for impact and social responsibility. Meanwhile, those models still maintain an increasing value of capital invested, not only the economic maximization based on purpose. This is a balance of investment and a sustainable green line we should follow.

3.3 The third outcome of this conference is building connections to facilitate the communication among investors, churches, government experts, academic institutions, etc. On the other side, it also means bridging the connections between different faith-based religions, such as Christian, Islam, Hindu, Buddhism, and other interfaith investors. Connections or cooperation for Africa now plays a big role to share experience, strengthen faith, drive investment and enhance social resilience.

3.4 The fourth outcome is the SDGs, mentioned in this conference and quite much previously. As we know during this COVID-19 period, we are facing or have faced many additional challenges. Nevertheless, keeping sight of the goals of our business activities even if they cannot immediately be reached, is already an amazing contribution. Let us commit ourselves or renew our commitment to the SDGs by crossing faith communities and other different sectors. Let us be motivated to think more carefully about the choices we make, mobilize capital and take action towards this direction.

3.5 The focus on credible faith communities is the fifth outcome of this conference. How can faith communities faithfully contribute to their valuos, and in turn be reliable or trustworthy for the investors? Faith communities must show their professional governance structures, data pool or some other competence needed for credible investments. Considering the aspects of the faith, it is also important to consult a variety of the different faiths to keep a broad perspective on objectives such as insight-driven strategies and actions, innovative services, experience-centricity by design, seamless interactions, responsive supply chain and operations, aligned and empowered workforce, digitally enabled technology architecture, and integrated partner and alliance ecosystem.

4

SUMMARY:
WALK THE TALK - ASIA FOCUS

It is hard to summarize a conference full of rich and professional input, as the summary can never completely cover all amazing ideas. However, some of the highlights are presented for better understanding and thus, easier to put into practice. This is also an opportunity to energize and explore further cooperation.

From late 2019, the global health emergency caused by COVID-19 has triggered an unprecedented economic shrink. However, the consequences from various aspects are potentially more harmful than the ones we are currently facing. People have begun to realize that we are all interconnected in the web of life and every single person's health will be tightly tied to the health of the whole community, even the whole world. The regulatory framework or legislation for social responsibility is another particularly important issue for the potential investors. Some of the Asian countries have managed impressive achievements on faith-based investments with suitable government regulation or legislation. For example, in the past few years, China's investments on alternative energy and infrastructures continue to grow at a large scale even during the onset of the pandemic in late 2019.

The consensus reached by the speakers was that the public parts, private sectors, academic institutions, churches, and other faith-based organizations should be highly encouraged to follow the SDGs to enhance social resilience, and more and more concrete faith-based investment should be stimulated for this sustainable purpose. To well actualize this purpose, collaboration on different levels and different aspects are highly needed. More technical assistance and information on sustainability are needed to enhance investors' capacity. We need a transition from traditional investment to impact investment which means the companies, organizations and funds, or other investors really need to have an intention to generate a measurable, beneficial social or environmental impact besides a financial return.

Some economic domains, such as the entertainment and retail sectors, have met the challenges of evolving client expectations through digital transformation. This need has allowed them to provide a seamless experience, while fundamentally changing the way their businesses operate.

This conference is meant to build bridges between the area of faith and the sector of investment. If we consider faith and values as the center along with three other dimensions (vertical, horizontal and time), then we may also say that it is the motivation, the motor or orientation across the whole presentation. Either in terms of its own domination or an economical perspective, or an interfaith perspective, this center is where we should act from.

Essentially, combined with the previous central point, the next central point is to make the link between faith and economy investment. How can our faith translate to business activities? One of the proposed efforts heard from the conference was to make faith more visible and more explicit in order to nurture these investment efforts.

Furthermore, the SDGs framework is an undoubtedly important point in the center and is also the key part of impact investment. Faith investment as a contribution to impact investment, and cannot be measured only by the financial returns but also by the social, political and sustainability returns. For example, in many of the Asian countries, climate transition strategies have been added to the agenda. The investing companies are leading this transition to zero carbon emission which is a part of climate resilience economy. To achieve success with this climate transition, the faith-based investors must embark on a journey in which they are essentially filling the crucial gap between the existing traditional mode and the mode of new clean tech of low carbon or zero carbon emission.

From the vertical dimension, the speakers started from the top level of macroeconomics and crossed to the low level of grassroots. The speakers were trying to figure out the relation between these two levels. A regulatory framework is needed on the ground level as many speakers mentioned. In the end, what we have done on the macroeconomic level will be measured and the impact in a person's real life will be evident. Even if we say there is a medium level of microeconomics between the macroeconomic level and the grassroots level, it falls within the whole range between top and bottom.

On the other side, in the horizontal dimension or spatial dimension, we see that the partnership is a keyboard. How can we align or cooperate with each other from different spatial locations? The partnership strategy, however, depends very much on the situation. In Asian countries for example, the percentage of the Christian population makes the partnership strategy quite different — such as in India and the Philippines, where the majority religion is entirely different. Concerning the needs for creating partnership, a concept of "stranded relationship" attracts our attention and is very meaningful as well. The concept defines how we can revitalize relationships and partnerships, which are somehow blocked for political, ideological or economic reasons.

The time dimension, as one of the three dimensions around the central concept "faith and values", is also a very valuable concept outcome from the conference. The concept "Run the Talk" was first mentioned by one of the speakers, Mr. Nicholas Niggli who is the deputy secretary general at Republic and Canton of Geneva. This indicates the time pressure and the necessity of speeding up the processes if we look at the speed of climate change. As we know, the faith communities have been dealing with these questions for thousands of years. The challenge here is how to find the right rhythm between speeding up and having long breath saving energy, with patience for a long run.

5

CONFERENCE RECOMMENDATIONS: ASIA FOCUS

As many speakers mentioned, we are facing the pandemic crisis worldwide. It poses different challenges for our daily life, especially traditional business activities. Meanwhile, this special situation also supplies us diverse opportunities in different areas, such as healthcare, agro-food and water, renewable energy and climate, education, finance and fintech, etc.

5.1 Enhancing the ***health and security*** aspects, developing the economic innovation and reducing the health gap between genders, rich and poor, geographic communities, are the main issues today. A collaborative approach of transforming and adapting the traditional management model to the new situation is much needed for these issues.

With this urgent need to transform the healthcare experience for patients and healthcare workers, the organizations can thrive under the new normal. Evidence from around the world shows that COVID-19 will provide the motivation for digital transformation and change the way that healthcare is delivered.[1] The new reality for healthcare requires the re-design of healthcare systems and introduction of new models to address primary, secondary and acute care as well as care that extends to the community.

5.2 Along with climate change, these issues of ***access to food and water*** are becoming more and more severe. How we address these chal-

---

[1]   https://www.healthcareitnews.com/news/emea/importance-connected-health-systems-post-covid-19-reality

lenges and how we make a success story about the challenges confronting investors in these areas, for example, the need to strengthen climate-responsive food and water governance structures. The rural communities or associations should be supported and provided with the related information to improve the agricultural ecosystem approaches, networking, financing, etc.

Some of the investment in the rural areas are strongly linked to other SDGs directly as well. For a concept of life enhancing, agriculture is a response to reclaim the ethical and spiritual dimensions to food and land which is marked by factorization. It promotes equitable economic relationships between and among producers, investors, traders and consumers.

5.3 *Renewable energy* production can significantly reduce reliance on diesel and gathered wood, the most polluting fuels. "It is the time to abandon our dependence on fossil fuels and move, quickly and decisively, towards forms of clean energy and a sustainable and circular economy. We have caused a climate emergency that gravely threatens nature and life itself, including our own," concludes Pope Francis, a leader of religious church.

Indeed, while the focus of religious investors has largely been on negative screening, there is a growing push for faith groups to become more proactive in making investments in asset classes considered to be socially responsible, including renewable energy.[2] We should encourage those valuable long-term investors that care both about attractive financial returns and the environment.

While this area is improving, there is a lack of information and awareness about the benefits and need of renewable energy. There is a clear need of related information from the public parts or other sectors. On the other hand, the pandemic has the potential to change the priority

---

[2]   https://www.windpowermonthly.com/article/1660455/putting-faith-renewable-energy

of government policies and budgets, developers' investment decisions and the availability of financing. The cost of the investment for renewable energy is also a challenge in most cases.

5.4 *Education*, as one of the most important SDGs, has been attracting global attention for decades. However, with the devastating impact of COVID-19, 95% of the students were disrupted due to school closures at all different levels. Education is facing new challenges worldwide. Certainly, faith-based cooperation can bring all our energies together to ensure that we address these challenges which have really been highlighted.

On the other side, education will influence the faith-based mindset which is crucial for following the entirety of the SDGs. Education plays a big role today on the faith side, especially when we are interconnected. Furthermore, education concerns and contributes more targets of sustainable development, such as human rights, gender equality, non-violence, appreciation of cultural diversity, etc.

5.5 *Fintech* means technology and innovation that aims to compete with traditional financial methods in the delivery of financial services. It is a vast new emerging industry that uses technology to improve activities in finance. However, it is also a challenge for some governments and banking organizations. The transformation of these challenges into opportunities and the integration of new technology with government efforts requires cooperation from both the public and private sector and is one of the efficient solutions which will drive us forward. Furthermore, the private sector and faith-based communities should work with government initiatives along with SDGs.

Rebuilding bridges in global governance, business and civil society around economic development, and different organizations that try to foster a systematic innovation shift mostly concerns sustainability and technology management.

APPENDICES

Conference Programme: Africa-Focus

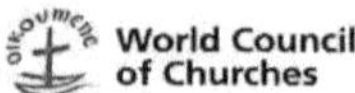   

4th International Faith-Based Investment Conference
Faith-Driven Investing: Walk the Talk
Africa-Europe Focus

Friday 15 January 2021, 9am – 5pm CET
Online on Conference Platform

Topic	*Covid-19 creates worldwide turbulences in health, economy, politics, education, religious answers and much more. Allocation of resources – capital, natural, human and religious resources – with the best impact on development becomes even more important. Churches and church-related partners and investors have great potential to contribute to faith-driven and impactful investing.* *After successful conferences in last three years on faith-driven investing, the focus of the conference 2021 is on Walk the talk by sharing experiences of successful and challenging investment projects, strengthening impactful cooperation between faith partners and investors, and present tools to make projects investable* *For reasons of time zones in online conferences, this one has a **Focus on Africa and Europe**. A similar conference is planned with **Focus on Asia on Friday 5 March 2021, subject to confirmation. More info follows on this website***
Fully Online	The conference will be held as virtual conference online, due to the global Covid-19 Pandemic and ongoing travel and meeting restrictions in Geneva.
Regis-tration	*Registration fee: 30 USD. See registration form. Please register until 10 January to plan the workgroups, but last-minute registration will remain open until 13 Jan. **Registration form and updates** on the programme on https://gafoundation.world/en/conference/conference-2021.*
Oikosinvest Partner Con-sultation	On Thursday 25 Feb, a workshop will be offered by Oikosinvest Foundation, the new foundation based in Geneva for faith-driven and values-driven investment with a consultation focussed on Africa. The workshop is offered on invitation only, for those who already submitted an investment application. For more information contact: stueckelberger@oikosinvest.org

Friday 15 January 2021	
Time CET	**Time East Africa: CET+2. Western Europe (UK) and West Africa: CET-1**
08.30–09.00	Login, chatroom open. "Networking Breakfast" (with your food at home 😊)
09.00–09.30	**1) Welcome.: Walk the Talk: Expectations for 2021. Plenary** • *Christoph Stückelberger*, Executive Director Geneva Agape Foundation GAF, Geneva • *Isabel Phiri*, Deputy General Secretary World Council of Churches, Geneva • *Nana Francois*, Director Membership, FaithInvest, Bristol/UK • *Timo Plutschinski*, Director WEA Business Coalition, Berlin/Germany • *Hong Bui*, GAF: Technical indications for breakout groups and bilateral talks.

09.30–10.10	**2) Keynotes Plenary** (Moderator Christoph Stückelberger)
	Setting the Scene: Impact and Faith drove Investing in and after the Corona Pandemic
	• *Anis Asghar, Investor, UK, Board Oikosinvest Foundation*
	  Needs, risks and opportunities of investing in Corona times. Investor perspective.
	• *Nkatha Njeru, Coordinator African Christian Health Association Platform ACHAP,*
	  Nairobi: Needs/ opportunities of health projects in Corona times. Church perspective.
	• *Bruno Bobone, new President of UNIAPAC:* The Contribution of Christian entrepreneurs
	  (Uniapac members) for Faith-driven Investments, with a focus on Africa.
	• *Roland Schatz, CEO UNGSII and President Geneva Agape Foundation, ev with Günter*
	  Nooke, Africa Desk of the Government of Germany, Berlin
	  Commitment of the German government for cooperation with faith-driven investing.

10.10–10.30	Networking Break with online bilateral encounter options.
10.30–11.45	**3) Working Session 5 parallel sessions with active interaction of participants.** Faith-driven Project Examples: one successful and one in consideration for investing • **Health** Sector (Moderator *Mwai Makoka*, WCC, Zambia/Geneva) • **Agro-food and water** sector (Moderator: *Athena Peralta*, WCC, Philippines/Geneva) • **Renewable Energy and Climate** sector (Moderator: *Timo Plutschinski*, WEA, Germany) • **Education** sector (Moderator: *Obiora Ike*, Globethics.net, Nigeria/Geneva) • **Financial and Fintech** sector (Moderator: *Nana Francois*, Faithinvest, UK) • **Real Estate / Infrastructure** (Moderator: *Chris Elisara*, WEA Creation Care, SDG Cities)
11.45–12.45	Lunch break, exhibition space. 10-15' bilateral networking slots with online reservation
12.45–14.00	**4) Plenary Panel and Discussion** (Moderator Nana Francois) **Loans, Interest Rates, Equities, Grants, Governance: What to consider** • *Jean-Pierre Sweerts, DOB Equity, Board Chairman, Kenya/Amsterdam, Board GAF* • *Oscar Iloh, Lombard Odier Private Bank, Geneva* • *Bright Mawudor, All Africa Conference of Churches, Deputy GS, Finance Director:* • *Nicholas Niggli, Deputy General Secretary Economic Development, State of Geneva,* *Canton of GenevaMember Building Bridges Initiative.*
14.00–14.45	**5) Plenary Panel and Discussion** (Moderator Lorna Gold) **Faiths Invest: Principles and Praxis in Islamic, Hindu and Interfaith Investments.** • *Omar Shaikh, Head Policy, Islamic Finance Council UKIFC, UK* • *Vivek Mittal, Hindu, CEO AFIDA (Africa Infrastructure Dev. Assoc.), India/London* • *Martin Palmer, CEO FaithInvest: Faith Long-term Plans. The strategy of FaithInvest.*
14.45–15.00	Networking Break with online bilateral encounter options.
15.00–16.00	**6) Plenary Panel and Discussion** (Moderator Christoph Stückelberger) **Making Investments Work. Three Cases.** • *Grant Smith, CEO Hand in Hand Group, Kenya/UK:* Affordable Housing • *Christopher Mbanefo, CEO Oxi-Zen, Continent Africa/Geneva:* CO2-Conversion Projects • *Ulrich Möller, President One Climate Fund, Germany/Southern Africa and Arumugam* *Pillay;* One Climate Fund Southern Africa.
16.–16.15	**7) Closing remarks, conclusion, follow up**
16.15–17.00	**8) Networking: Online Bilateral Contacts on the Conference Platform**

Conference Programme: Asia-Focus

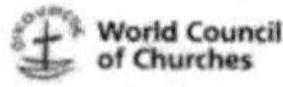

4th International Faith-Based Investment Conference Online
Faith-Driven Investing: Walk the Talk
Asia Focus

Friday 5 March 2021, 9.00am – 5.00pm IST (India)
11.30am CST (China/Phil.), 4.30am CET (Europe), 3.30am UTC (UK), 10.30pm EST

Topic
Covid-19 creates worldwide turbulences in health, economy, politics, education, religious answers and much more. Allocation of resources – capital, natural, human and religious resources – with the best impact on development becomes even more important. Churches and church-related partners and investors have great potential to contribute to faith-driven and impactful investing.
After successful conferences in last three years on faith-driven investing, the focus of the conference 2021 is on *Walk the talk* by sharing experiences of successful and challenging investment projects, strengthening impactful cooperation between faith partners and investors, and present tools to make projects investable
For reasons of time zones in online conferences, this one has a **Focus on Asia**. A similar conference was held on 15 January with the Focus on **Africa**

Fully Online
The conference will be held as virtual conference online, due to the global Covid-19 Pandemic and ongoing travel and meeting restrictions in Geneva. The plenary sessions will be available as video after the conference on the conference page below. Those from the Africa Focus conference held on 15 January are already available there.

Registration
Registration fee: 30 USD. See registration form. Registration is open until 4 March, but please register earlier to plan the workgroups and for participants to find you in advance. **Registration form and updates** on the programme on
https://gafoundation.world/en/conference/conference-2021

Friday 5 March 2021	
Time India	**11.30am CST (China), 12.30.am KST, 4.30am CET (Europe),3.30am UTC**
08.30-09.00	Login, chatroom open, "Networking Breakfast" (with your food at home ☺)
09.00-09.30	**1) Welcome: Walk the Talk: Expectations for 2021. Plenary** • *Christoph Stückelberger*, Executive Director Geneva Agape Foundation GAF, Geneva • *Isabel Phiri*, Deputy General Secretary World Council of Churches, Geneva • *Nana Francois*, Director Membership, FaithInvest, Bristol/UK • *Timo Plutschinski*, Director WEA Business Coalition, Berlin/Germany • *Hong Bui*, GAF: Technical indications for breakout groups and bilateral talks.
09.30-10.20	**2) Keynotes Plenary** (Moderator Christoph Stückelberger) **Setting the Scene: Impact and Faith-driven Investing in and after the Corona Pandemic** • *Anis Asghar, Investor, UK/Bangladesh, Board Oikosinvest Foundation* Needs, risks and opportunities of investing in Corona times. Investor perspective. • *Mathews George Chunakara, General Secretary, Christian Conference of Asia*, Thailand/India: Needs and opportunities of investing in Asian church-related programmes. • *Baocheng Liu, Professor of Business Ethics, Beijing/China, Advisor to the government on China-Africa-Investments*: Social Responsibility in Chinese Outbound Investments. • *Prune Ansvananda, President of UNIAPAC Asia, Thailand*: The Contribution of Christian entrepreneurs (Uniapac members) for Faith-driven Investments, with a focus on Asia
10.20-10.40	Networking Break with online bilateral encounter options.
10.40-11.45	**3) Working Session 6 parallel sessions with active interaction of participants.** Faith-driven Project Examples: one successful and one in consideration for investing • **Health** Sector (Moderator *Manoj Kurian*, India/Geneva, WCC, Public Health Expert • **Agro-food and water** sector (Moderator: *Athena Peralta*, WCC, Philippines/Geneva) • **Renewable Energy and Climate** sector (Moderator: *Timo Plutschinski*, WEA, Germany) • **Education** sector (Moderator: *Asha Singh Kanvar*, President Common Wealth of Learning CoL. • **Financial and Fintech** sector (Moderator: *Nana Francois*, Faithinvest, UK) • **Real Estate / Infrastructure** (Moderator: *Chris Elisara*, WEA Creation Care, SDG Cities)
11.45-12.45	Lunch break, exhibition space, 10-15' bilateral networking slots with online reservation
12.45-14.00	**4) Plenary Panel and Discussion** (Moderator Nana Francois) **Loans, Interest Rates, Equities, Grants, Governance: What to consider** • *Nicolas Karambadzakis, ECLOF International, Geneva.* Microcredits • *Mason Tan, Founder Garden Impact Investments, Singapore*: Investing in the poor. • *Jean-Pascal Beyrard, Partner, Lombard Odier Private Bank, Geneva*: Impact Investing as a private bank. • *Nicholas Niggli, Deputy General Secretary Economic Development, State of Geneva, Canton of Geneva*, Member Building Bridges Initiative: Asian Investment Bridges.
14.00-14.45	**5) Plenary Panel and Discussion** (Moderator Lorna Gold) **Faiths Invest: Principles and Praxis in Islamic, Hindu and Interfaith Investments.** • *Vivek Mittal, Hindu, CEO AFIDA (Africa Infrastructure Dev. Assoc.), India/London.* • *Martin Palmer, CEO FaithInvest: Faith Long-term Plans.* The strategy of FaithInvest. • *Mizue Tsukushi*, President & CEO of Good Bankers Japan & *Michael Shackleton*, FaithInvest Consultant for Asia: Building on traditional values: examples from Japan
14.45-15.00	Networking Break with online bilateral encounter options.
15.00-16.00	**6) Plenary Panel and Discussion** (Moderator Christoph Stückelberger) **Making Investments Work. Three Cases.** • *Nawang Kunphel, Ladak, India*: Pennees Row Project • *Joy Cadangen, Philippines/Geneva, Board Oikosinvest*: Affordable Housing • *Christopher Mbanefo, CEO Oxï-Zen, Global/Geneva*: CO2-Conversion Projects
16.-16.15	**7) Closing remarks, conclusion, follow up**
16.15-17.00	**8) Networking: Online Bilateral Contacts on the Conference Platform**

List of Speakers and Participants
from Conference Africa-Focus

Surname	First Name	Organisation	Email
Asghar	Anis	OikosInvest Foundation	Anis @clancapital.co.uk
Bobone	Bruno	International Christian Union of Business Executives UNIAPAC	President @uniapac.org
Iloh	Oscar	Lombard Odier Private Bank	o.iloh @lombardodier.com
Elisara	Chris	World Evangelical Alliance WEA	Celisara @worldea.org
Francois	Nana	FaithInvest	nana.francois @faithinvest.org
Gold	Lorna	FaithInvest	lorna.gold @faithinvest.org
Ike	Obiora	Globethics.net	Ike@globethics.net
Makoka	Mwai	World Council of Churches WCC	Mwai.Makoka @wcc-coe.org
Mawudor	Bright	All Africa Conference of Churches AACC	Mawudor @aacc-ceta.org
Mbanefo	Christopher	OXÏ-ZEN	chris@oxi-zen
Mittal	Vivek	Africa Infrastructure Development Association AfIDA	vivek.mittal @afida-africa.org
Möller	Ulrich	One Climate Fund	dr.moeller @lka.ekvw.de
Niggli	Nicholas	Deputy General Secretary Economic Development, State	Nicholas.Niggli @etat.ge.ch

Surname	First Name	Organisation	Email
		of Geneva	
Njeru	Nkatha	African Christian Health Association ACHA	Coordinator @africachap.org
Nooke	Günter	Africa Desk of the Government of Germany	guenter.nooke @bmz.bund.de
Palmer	Martin	FaithInvest	martin.palmer @faithinvest.org
Peralta	Athena	World Council of Churches WCC	Athena.Peralta @wcc-coe.org
Phiri	Isabel	World Council of Churches WCC	Isabel.Phiri @wcc-coe.org
Pillay	Arumugam	One Climate Fund	pillaymorgan17 @gmail.com
Plutschinski	Timo	World Evangelical Alliance WEA	timo.plutschinski @worldea.org
Schatz	Roland	UN Global Sustainability Index Institute Foundation UNGSII	roland.schatz @ungsii.org
Shaikh	Omar	Islamic Finance Council UKIFC	omar@ukifc.com
Smith	Grant	Hand in Hand Group	Grant @handinhandgroup. com
Stückel-berger	Christoph	Geneva Agape Foundation	Stueckelberger @gafoundation. world
Sweerts	Jean-Pierre	DOB Equity, Geneva Agape Foundation	jp@sweerts.eu

List of Speakers and Participants
from Conference Asia-Focus

Surname	First Name	Organisation	Email
Ansvananda	Prune	International Christian Union of Business Executives UNIAPAC Asia	prune.ansvananda@gmail.com
Asghar	Anis	OikosInvest Foundation	Anis@clancapital.co.uk
Baocheng	Liu	Center for International Business Ethics CIBE	baocheng.liu@gmail.com
Beyrard	Jean-Pascal	Lombard Odier	jp.beyrard@lombardodier.com
Cadangen	Joy	OikosInvest Foundation	Cadangen@gafoundation.world
Chunakara	Mathews George	Christian Conference of Asia	Ccagensec@gmail.com
Elisara	Chris	World Evangelical Alliance Creation Care Task Force	Celisara@worldea.org
Francois	Nana	FaithInvest	nana.francois@faithinvest.org
Gold	Lorna	FaithInvest	lorna.gold@faithinvest.org
Karambadzakis	Nicolas	ECLOF International	Karambadzakis@web.de
Kunphel	Nawang	Monk, Monastery Ladakh, India	Nkunphel@gmail.com
Kurian	Manoj	World Council of Churches WCC	manoj.kurian@wcc-coe.org
Mbanefo	Christopher	OXÏ-ZEN	Chris@oxi-zen.io
Mittal	Vivek	Africa Infrastructure Development Association AFIDA	vivek.mittal@afida-africa.org

Surname	First Name	Organisation	Email
Niggli	Nicholas	Deputy Secretary General at the Republic and State of Geneva	Nicholas.Niggli @etat.ge.ch
Palmer	Martin	FaithInvest	martin.palmer @faithinvest.or g
Peralta	Athena	World Council of Churches WCC	athena.peralta @wcc-coe.org
Phiri	Isabel	World Council of Churches WCC	isabel.phiri @wcc-coe.org
Plutschinski	Timo	World Evangelical Alliance WEA	timo.plutschins ki @worldea.org
Shackleton	Michael	Osaka Gakuin University	Michaelshack-leton @yahoo.co.uk
Singh Kanvar	Asha	Commonwealth of Learning COL	Akanwar @col.org
Stückel-berger	Christoph	Geneva Agape Foundation	Stueckelberger @gafoundation. world
Tan	Mason	Garden Impact Investments Pte Ltd GII	Mason @gardenimpact .com
Tsukushi	Mizue	The Good Bankers Co.,Ltd.	Secr @goodbankers. co.jp
Urban	Michael	Lombard Odier	m.urban @lombardodier. com

Photo Gallery

Christopher Mbanefo, CH

Günter Nooke, Germany

Lorna Gold, UK

Martin Palmer, UK

Bruno Bobone, Portugal

Grant Smith, UK

Oscar Iloh, CH

Jean-Pierre Sweerts, NL

Arumugam Pillay, South Africa

Bright Mawudor, Kenya

Ulrich Möller, Germany

Roland Schatz, CH

Nicholas Niggli, CH

Nkatha Njeru, Kenya

Haicun Kong, China

Omar Shaikh, UK

Christoph Stückelberger, CH

Anis Asghar, United Kingdom

Isabel Phiri, Switzerland

Prune Ansvananda, Thailand

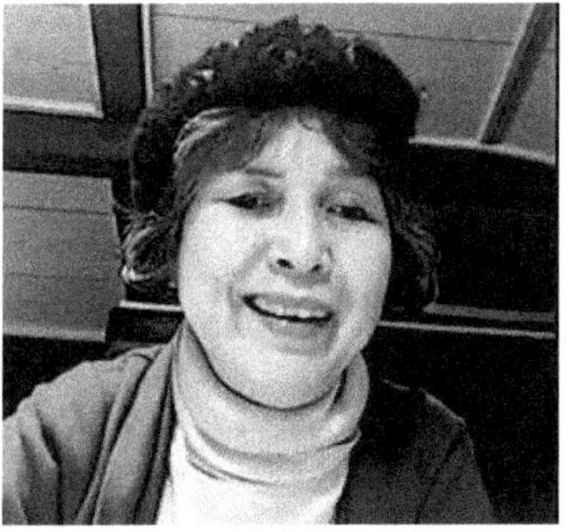

Mizue Tsukushi, Japan

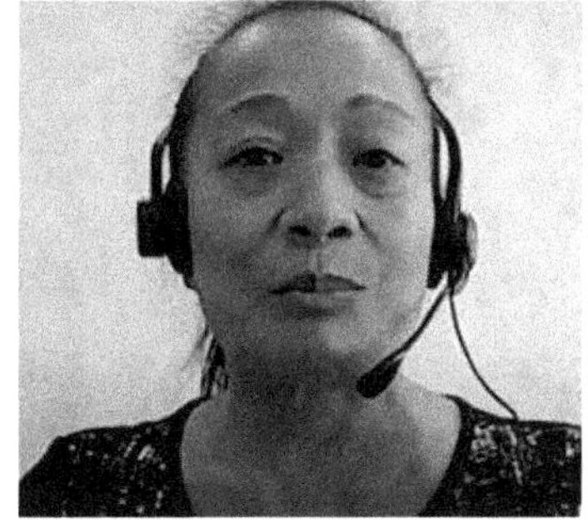

Joy Cadangen, Switzerland

Nicolas Karambadzakis, CH

Mathews Chunakara, TH

Hong Bui-Rydell, Switzerland

Athena Peralta, Switzerland

Michael Shackleton, Japan

Mason Tan, Singapore

Vivek Mittal, United Kingdom

Nawang Kunphel, India

Timo Plutschinski, Germany

Liu Baocheng, China

Michael Urban, Switzerland

Nana Francois, UK

The Geneva Agape Foundation (GAF) is an international non-profit organisation, based in Geneva/Switzerland. It assists faith and non-faith organisations in three programmes:

- Values-driven Entrepreneurship
- Research, Publications, Philanthropy
- Values-driven Investments

The Foundation provides publications, trainings, consultancy service and investment projects. Its Annual International Conference in Geneva gives an opportunity to values driven organisations to share knowledge, being stronger together and make bridges between investors and investee. GAF has a good cooperation with partners in China and an international Board of Foundation. Its mission is serving communities with love, transparency and accountability.

www.gafoundation.world

Globethics.net is an ethics network of teachers and institutions based in Geneva, with an international Board of Foundation and with ECOSOC status with the United Nations. Our vision is to embed ethics in higher education. In order to ensure access to knowledge resources in applied ethics, Globethics.net has developed four resources:

Globethics.net Library & Globethics.net Publications

The leading global digital library on ethics and a publishing house open to all the authors interested in applied ethics.

Globethics.net Academy & Globethics.net Network

Online and offline courses and training for all on ethics and a global network of experts and institutions including a Pool of experts and a Consortium

www.globethics.net ∎

Globethics.net Publications

The list below is only a selection of our publications. To view the full collection, please visit our website.

All free products are provided free of charge and can be downloaded in PDF form from the Globethics.net library and at www.globethics.net/publications. Bulk print copies can be ordered from *publications@globethics.net* at special rates from the Global South.
Paid products not provided free of charge are indicated *
The Editor of the different Series of Globethics.net Publications Prof. Dr. Obiora Ike, Executive Director of Globethics.net in Geneva and Professor of Ethics at the Godfrey Okoye University Enugu/Nigeria.

Contact for manuscripts and suggestions: *publications@globethics.net*

Agape Series

崔万田 Cui Wantian 爱+经济学 *Agape Economics*, 2020, 420pp. ISBN: 978-2-88931-349-5

Cui Wantian, Christoph Stückelberger, *The Better Sinner: A Practical Guide on Corruption*, 2020, 37pp. ISBN: 978-2-88931-339-6. Available also in Chinese.

Anh Tho Andres Kammler, *FaithInvest: Impactful Cooperation. Report of the International Conference Geneva 2020*, 2020, 70pp. ISBN: 978-2-88931- 357-0

崔万田 Cui Wantian, 价值观创造价值 企业家信仰于企业绩效 *Values Create Value. Impact through Faith-based Entrepreneurship*, 2020, 432pp. IBSN: 978-2-88931-361-7

Moses C. 编辑, 圣商灵粮：中国基督徒企业家的灵修日记 *Daily Bread for Christians in Business: The Spiritual Diary of Chinese Christian Entrepreneurs*, 412pp. 2021, ISBN 978-2-88931-391-4

Haicun Kong, *Walk the Talk. Africa / Asia Focus. Report of the International Online Conference, Jan / Mar 2021*, 2021, 41pp. ISBN 978-2-88931- 411-9

China Christian Series

Spirituality 4.0 at the Workplace and FaithInvest - Building Bridges, 2019, 107pp. ISBN 978-2-88931-304-4

海茵兹·吕格尔 / 克里斯多夫·芝格里斯特 (Christoph Sigrist/ Heinz Rüegger) *Diaconia: An Introduction. Theological Foundation of Christian Service*, 2019, 433pp. ISBN: 978-2-88931-302-0

Faith-Based Entrepreneurs Stronger Together. Report of the International Conference Geneva 2018, 2018, 86pp. ISBN: 978-2-88931-258-0

China Ethics Series

Liu Baocheng/Chandni Patel, *Overseas Investment of Chinese Enterprises. A Casebook on Corporate Social Responsibility*, forthcoming 2020, ISBN: 978-2-88931-355-6.

Liu Baocheng / Zhang Mengsha, *CSR Report on Chinese Business Overseas Operations*, 2018, 286pp. ISBN: 978-2-88931-250-4

刘宝成（Liu Baocheng）/ 张梦莎（Zhang Mengsha），中国企业"走出去"社会责任研究报告, 2018, 267pp. ISBN: 978-2-88931-248-1

Liu Baocheng / Zhang Mengsha, *Philanthropy in China: Report of Concepts, History, Drivers, Institutions*, 2017, 246pp. ISBN: 978–2–88931–178–1

Focus Series

Cristina Calvo, Humberto Shikiya, Deivit Montealegre (Eds.), *Ética y economía: la relación dañada. Profundizando los modos de un auténtico desarrollo humano integral sostenible (Parte II)*, 2020, 311pp. ISBN : 978-2-88931-347-1

Ruth Dymphna Maduforo, *Domestic Violence - Ethical Challenges to the Professionalism of Religious and Faith Leaders for Healing Survivors*, 2020, 85pp. ISBN 978-2-88931-314-9

Murhega Mashanda / Kitoka Moke, *Opportunités et défis de la réconciliation à l'Est de la République démocratique du Congo*, 2020, 63pp. ISBN 978-2-88931-325-9

Bosco Muchukiwa Rukakiza, *Résilience et transformation des conflits dans les États des Grands Lacs africains: Théorie, démarches et applications*, 2021, 126pp. ISBN 978-2-88931-405-8

Theses Series

Florence Muia, *Sustainable Peacebuilding Strategies*, 2020, 205pp. ISBN 978-2-88931-331-0

Mary Rose-Claret Ogbuehi, *The Struggle for Women Empowerment Through Education,* 2020, 410pp. ISBN: 978-2-88931-363-1

Nestor Engone Elloué, *La justice climatique restaurative: Réparer les inégalités Nord/Sud*, 2020, 198pp. ISBN 978-2-88931-379-2

Hilary C. Ike, *Organizational Improvement of Nigerian Catholic Chaplaincy in Central Ohio*, 2021, 154pp. ISBN 978-2-88931-385-3

Education Ethics Series

Obiora Ike, Justus Mbae, Chidiebere Onyia, Herbert Makinda (Eds.), *Mainstreaming Ethics in Higher Education Vol. 2*, 2021, 420pp. ISBN: 978-2-88931-383-9

Christoph Stückelberger/ Joseph Galgalo/ Samuel Kobia (Eds.), *Leadership with Integrity. Higher Education from Vocation to Funding*, 2021, 288pp. ISBN 978-2-88931-389-1

African Law Series

Pascal Mukonde Musulay, *Droits, libertés et devoirs de la personne et des peuples en droit international africain Tome I Promotion et protection*, 282pp. 2021, ISBN 978-2-88931-397-6

Pascal Mukonde Musulay, *Droits, libertés et devoirs de la personne et des peuples en droit international africain Tome II Libertés, droits et obligations démocratiques*, 332pp. 2021, ISBN 978-2-88931-399-0

Ambroise Katambu Bulambo, *Règlement judiciaire des conflits électoraux. Précis de droit comparé africain*, 2021, 672pp., ISBN 978-2-88931-403-4

Co-publications & Other

Obiora F. Ike, *Applied Ethics to Issues of Development, Culture, Religion and Education*, 2020, 280pp. ISBN 978-2-88931-335-8

Obiora F. Ike, *Moral and Ethical Leadership, Human Rights and Conflict Resolution – African and Global Contexts*, 2020, 191pp. ISBN 978-2-88931-333-4

Kenneth R. Ross, *Mission Rediscovered: Transforming Disciples*, 2020, 138pp. ISBN 978-2-88931-369-3

Obiora Ike, Amélé Adamavi-Aho Ekué, Anja Andriamay, Lucy Howe López (Eds.), *Who Cares About Ethics?* 2020, 352pp. ISBN 978-2-88931-381-5

This is only selection of our latest publications, to view our full collection please visit:

www.globethics.net/publications